The Original Simple Mom's Idea Book

Hints and Hacks for Home and Family

DEBORAH TAYLOR-HOUGH

DEBORAH TAYLOR-HOUGH

Copyright © 2015 Deborah Taylor-Hough

(Previously published as *The Simple Mom's Idea Book* – 2007)

Simple Pleasures Press
Auburn Washington USA

ISBN-13: 978-0692442289
ISBN-10: 0692442286

DEDICATION

This book is dedicated to my blog readers, Facebook followers, ezine subscribers, and other readers throughout the world. You've continually made my online life a joy.

CONTENTS

INTRODUCTION

In case you don't know who I am, my friends call me Debi, and you can, too. I'm an author, freelance writer, speaker, editor, full-time Graduate student, and mom to three adult children. And I've been doing this whole frugal, simple living thing for a long time.

Nearly three decades ago, our family bucked the tide of late-20th Century American life. We became a one income family in a two income world. We set out on a journey toward frugal living and simplicity that quickly became an education in itself—and a rewarding, joy-filled lifestyle. Through hard work and determination, our family paid off outstanding consumer debt and medical bills, radically reduced spending in every area of our lives, and most importantly, lived to tell about it!

During our family's lean times, we learned creative ways to stretch our limited finances while not sacrificing our quality of life. I began sharing what I've learned on blogs, websites, discussion forums, and eventually in books and magazines, as well. In many ways, this book is the book I wish I'd had when I was first starting out as a young wife and mother with little idea of how to stretch a penny until it screams. Someone told me, "Write the book you needed to read." So—to keep a long story short—I wound up writing a number of them.

You can find information about my other titles at the back of this book. I don't claim to be an expert on all things frugal or simple, but I wish I hadn't needed to learn this the hard way. Here's your chance to avoid getting an honorary Home Economics degree from the University of Hard Knocks. ☺

Debi Taylor-Hough
Seattle 2015

1

SIMPLIFYING PHONE CALLS AT HOME

When I was growing up, my mom always kept a list of frequently called phone numbers taped onto the telephone stand in the kitchen. That way we always had easy access to those numbers we called so often, the phone book almost opened to their page naturally.

But, silly me, I never bothered taking the time to do the same thing in my own home until my kids were in their teens. I just kept my personal address/phone book next to the phone in the kitchen, and then thumbed through it quickly whenever I needed a number. This system "worked" … but it was rather frustrating if someone walked off with my phone book to use it in another room, and then forgot to return it to its "home" in the kitchen.

Eventually I was inspired to make up a list of those frequently called numbers. I typed it up on the computer and printed out three copies, one to keep by each phone in the house. I used the computer so that if anyone on the list changes phone numbers or I need to add a new number or category to the list, I can just quickly update the information in the computer file, and then print out three new copies.

I've taped each phone number list onto the wall right next to each phone so that the lists don't grow legs and walk away—with three active kids in the house, things always seem to be finding their way to other parts of the house where they don't belong.

I kept our list fairly short because in an emergency I didn't want one of my kids having trouble finding a number lost amid all the others. I also didn't include friends' numbers because usually only one person in the family would be calling each of those numbers. The listed numbers are the ones that all five of us might have need to call on a regular basis.

The types of numbers I included are:

- The number to access Voice Messaging
- Family numbers (work, grandparents)
- Emergency neighborhood contact
- Frequently called professionals (doctors, church, vet, etc.)
- Our home address*
- Our home phone number*

*I included our home address and phone number on this

list because in the midst of an emergency, it can be challenging to remember vital details like phone numbers and addresses.

I was amazed at how happy everyone in the family was with this simple change! When my kids needed to call Grandpa, there's no fumbling around through the phone book. The numbers we need are there in front of us, right where we need them.

It's great!

Here are a few tips sent in from readers of my email newsletter, Simple Times, about this way of simplifying phone calls:

"Another great reason for this seemingly simple idea is: I was at my in-laws one Thanksgiving when the neighbor had a heart attack. My hubby, mother-in-law, and father-in-law all ran over there—leaving me at my in-laws to call911. I didn't know their address!! It might not even be a family member making the call!"

—JoAnne

"I have been doing the same thing for years. But I also have a second page with the numbers of businesses that we deal with. That page only goes with the kitchen phone. I also keep a copy of the first page in my purse, one in the cell phone case, and one in the car's glove compartment."

—Carole

"I even made mine miniature-sized to put in my purse.

Love it, love it!!"
    —*Cindy S.*

"Another idea that works with phone numbers. I keep a little index file with phone numbers listed in alphabetical order. It works well without cluttering the walls. You could put the emergency number on a card at the front of the box. One advantage of this is that the phone numbers and addresses, e-mail and cell phone numbers can be changed easily, and then the index card can just be thrown away. It has worked for us anyway."
    —*No name given*

"I have some tips about phone lists by your telephone. If you have speed dial on your phone, be sure to include those numbers on your printed list. The phones can lose their memory (especially if it uses batteries). Imagine a child trying to call Grandma for help and the speed dial button doesn't work. Having your full name, phone number (including area code) and address on every telephone in your house is a good safety tip. You know the information but your children's friends or house guests may not! Finally, having a steno pad with an attached pen next to each phone is a great help. Not just for messages but for anything else you need to note when you are on the phone. They are also a great resource for your family. Packs of steno pads are very cheap and last a long time. I wouldn't be without them."
    —*Mary*

2

SAVING ON HOME HEATING AND ELECTRIC COSTS

According to studies I've read, approximately 40% of winter home energy bills involve heating-related expenses. Here are some simple tips for cutting back on your home energy costs this winter:

Heating:

- Change furnace air filters regularly (once a month or according to the manufacturer's recommendations).
- Schedule a cleaning/maintenance call each year for your furnace.
- Install a programmable thermostat.

- Turn down the heat one degree during the day. Lower the heat by ten degrees at night.
- Make sure your furniture and carpets don't cover or block vents or air ducts.

Insulating:

- Add weather-stripping around doors and windows.
- Install thermo-pane windows in your home.
- Insulate your top floor ceilings and attic.
- Replace window screens with storm windows.
- Close the damper on the chimney flue when not in use.
- Cover your windows with insulated blinds or curtains. Or make window quilts for the winter months.
- Insulate yourself! Wear a sweater and insulated slippers in the house. Buy a down comforter for your bed.

Lighting:

- Use compact florescent lights, especially in outside lighting like porch lights that are left on for long periods of time.

- Use photo-cells or motion sensors for outdoor lights.
- Open drapes when the sun is shining in your windows (helps to provide both light and passive heat), and be sure to remember to close the drapes at night to keep the heat in.
- Turn off lights when you leave a room.
- Appliances:
- Insulate your older water heater.
- General rule of thumb: If you aren't using it, turn it off!
- Unplug electronics and electric appliances when not in use (battery chargers, hair appliances, computers).
- Use a power strip as a central turn off point for electronics, videos games, and computers when not in use.
- Use the right size pot on the stovetop.

Cleaning:

- Always run full loads of both laundry and dishes.
- If you have a newer model dishwasher, don't rinse dishes prior to putting them in the dishwasher.
- Install an energy efficient showerhead which will not only save on water usage, but also save money on water heating.

- Wash clothes in cold water whenever possible. Hot water heating uses 90% of the electricity used to run your washing machine.
- Use the correct water level when washing clothes.
- Don't over-dry your clothes. Hang to dry—or to finish drying—whenever possible.
- Empty your lint trap before each load.

3

KEEPING YOUR SUMMERTIME ORGANIZED

Just because life is a bit more relaxed during the lazy days of summer doesn't change the fact that we still need to know where things are and keep them handy. Here are some simple tips to keep your summertime activities and supplies running smoothly.

1) Keep like items grouped together in separate crates: BBQ supplies, pool maintenance supplies, etc.

2) Keep a basket of beach towels clean and rolled up in the laundry room near the outside door for easy pool, lake, beach, sprinkler, play.

3) Keep a handled bin in the back of your trunk or van for putting supplies, groceries, etc. and keeping them from rolling all over the car.

4) Have an insulated bag rolled up in the trunk, too, for keeping frozen foods cold on the trip home from the store on hot days.

5) Keep a folded blanket or sturdy tablecloth in the back of the car for impromptu picnics in the park, or to sit on during an outdoor theater or concert event.

6) Store all hand-held gardening and weeding tools in plastic bucket with a handle. Trowel, gloves, knee pad, etc.

7) Hang a shoe-bag organizer over the back of one of the car's front seats for your kids to store their toys, books, games, maps, water bottle, and other car or travelling related supplies. If the bag's too long, cut it to length and hem the bottom.

8) In your guest bathroom, keep a small bin or wooden box on the countertop for easy access with a collection of summertime ointments and lotions. Sunscreen (a variety of SPF levels), aloe, hand lotion, bug spray/lotion, antiseptic, anti-itch lotion for bug bites.

9) Store a small accordion file in your car with all essential car-related stuff. Registration, insurance information, maps, emergency contacts, receipts, and directions.

10) Store a "Before We Leave" checklist in luggage. Make a master list of chores, errands, and packing requirements you encounter before each out of town trip you make. You can even laminate the list and then check off complete items with a dry erase marker.

11) Before leaving on your summer road trip, make certain that your jumper cables, tire jack, and emergency kit are all actually in the car.

12) Keep all camping supplies in one place. Store camping cookware in a hamper that stays packed and ready to go at a moment's notice. A Camper's Word to the Wise: If you're going tent camping, double-check your tent poles are actually packed with the rest of the tent before you find yourself attempting to set up camp in the mountains—miles and miles from civilization—without tent poles. Please don't ask how I know this one.

4

SIMPLIFYING PARTY PLANNING

Hosting a party doesn't need to be an event just for holidays. Most people already have full calendars around major holidays, but are actually grateful for an invitation to a special gathering at an otherwise quiet time of year.

Maybe you and your guests would enjoy a big Mexican-themed celebration for Cinco de Mayo, a brunch on the Fourth of July before going to the local festivals or parades, or a special Valentine's Day dessert party.

Whether you're looking to have a simple family dinner party, a gathering for friends, or a major reunion, here are some simple tips to keep your party fun-filled for both you and your guests—without breaking the bank!

Type of Party

The first step for planning a successful party is to decide what type of gathering you want to host. Full-fledge sit down dinner parties are probably what comes to mind first when thinking of gatherings but there are other easier and less expensive options.

For ease of preparation, consider a buffet-style dinner rather than a seated dinner party. For a buffet, be sure to select foods that don't require cutting with a knife or are covered with runny sauces that could drip onto clothes or carpets as people mingle.

Potluck dinners work well for large gatherings: family celebrations, reunions, church activities, gatherings of close friends. If you're hosting a potluck, you might want to suggest items for people to bring. An easy way to divide up the food preparation is to include a note with your invitation that states: Families with last names starting with the letters "A-H" bring side dishes/salads, "I-Q" bring main dishes, and "R-Z" bring desserts. You'll be taking "potluck" about which actual food items people choose to prepare but by dividing up the general categories ahead of time, you'll be assured that the basics are covered. As the host, you'll need to provide serving utensils, silverware, plates and drinks.

For a fun party alternative to a full dinner consider throwing an appetizer party or a dessert buffet.

Many parties move from being simple gatherings to fun-filled events by the addition of a theme. Here are some possibilities: birthday, anniversary, holiday, casino night, roaring 20's, road rally, rock star costume party, toga party, crab feed, 50's sock hop, garden party, luau, scavenger hunt, Mardi Gras, magic, science fiction, Mad Hatter's tea party, tropical, 60's retro, disco, movie stars, masquerade, Wild West barbecue. Many of these themes work equally well with both children and adult parties.

Sometimes the sillier the theme, the more fun—especially for adults who may need to loosen up a bit and smile more often. For example, rather than hosting a simple backyard barbecue this summer, throw a Cowboy Barbecue. Ask people to arrive wearing their own selection of blue jeans or jean skirts, western looking shirts, colorful bandanas, cowboy hats, boots. Serve steak sandwiches, hot dogs for the kids, coleslaw, baked beans and cornbread on picnic tables (or even hay bales!) covered with red and white checked tablecloths. For entertainment, play country music, teach everyone some simple line dances and stage a horseshoe throwing contest. If the barbecue goes into the evening hours after dark, end the party with a campfire and old-fashioned sing along.

Planning Ahead

The simplest and most important trick for saving time, effort and money on your party is to plan ahead. A small notebook or three-ring binder can be used for your personal planning notebook, keeping track of all the big (and small!) details of your event. You can also keep your notebook for future events.

A planning notebook is a step that professional party planners use to keep track of the variety of details involved with a party, and it also helps the host/hostess stick to a predetermined budget.

Using dividers, separate your Party Notebook into the following six sections:

1. The Basics
2. The Budget
3. The Guest List
4. The Menu
5. Preparation Lists
6. Decorations

In your Party Notebook, you'll want to include any and all steps needed for accomplishing everything for your party. Break down the steps into weeks, days and hours before your event. List even obvious details such as "set out the silverware," since these tend to be the sort of things that can often get overlooked in the rush.

1) The Basics

This section includes a list of the basic details of your party: the date, time and location. Be sure to included detailed instructions to the party location, providing a map if available. The date of the event doesn't have to be actually on the event date that you're celebrating. For example, having an anniversary celebration the day after big day allows the anniversary couple the joy of celebrating just the two of them and also sharing their celebration with their friends and family.

When planning when to send invitations, be sure to allow plenty of time for people to arrange their schedules, usually at least three weeks in advance. Remember, for outdoor parties plan a contingency in case of inclement weather.

2) The Budget

Plan an estimated budget beforehand for all expenses, keeping a running total as you shop and prepare. As you're shopping for your party, always shop from a detailed list with an estimated idea of what you should be spending. One simple way to save money on party products is by using the good china and silverware (if you have it) rather than paper plates, plastic tableware, etc. This might add a bit more work afterwards with clean-up, but it brings a simple touch of elegance to your gathering.

3) Guest List

Include in this section of your notebook the names, addresses, phone numbers, RSVP record, special dietary requirements.

4) Menu

Include everything from beverages to appetizers to

desserts.

An important thing to remember when planning your menu is: "Know your guests." Find out if anyone avoids alcohol or has special dietary requirements or food allergies. Many older people can't eat rich or spicy foods. Are your guests sophisticated gourmets or more comfortable with familiar favorites?

If children will be attending your party, include some simple child-friendly foods in your menu (for example, red gelatin salad with sliced bananas is always a hit with kids).

Aim for balance in your menu. And remember, foods don't have to be expensive to be tasty. Simply adding fresh herbs from your garden as a garnish can often be enough to dress up less-expensive recipes.

Select recipes that are easy to prepare or can be made ahead of time. Consider food that the guests help prepare such as salad bar, baked potato bar, etc.

Don't try a new recipe for the first time at a party, use your tried and true favorites.

One of the simplest tricks for easy party planning is to make as many food items ahead of time as possible. Many foods can be prepared, frozen, and then thawed and reheated on party day with a minimal amount of effort. The following items freeze well: cookies, cakes, casseroles, main dishes, side dishes, appetizers, desserts.

5) Preparation Lists

This section of your notebook includes a list of the

step by step preparation for every sub-section of your party plan. Be sure to plan out individual preparation lists for these topics: cleaning and preparing the house, checking for supplies and equipment, cooking, decorating, shopping.

6) Decorations

Think through every room that guests will be using and then decide if you want to include special decorations in each room. Be sure to consider table and food service decor, room decorations, yard, front door, bathroom, etc. When it comes to decorations, simpler is often better. Too many decorations can overwhelm your budget and also make a crowd room look too busy. A seasonal wreath on the door, candles scattered around the house, and a flower arrangement on the table could be all you need to make the house look festive.

For centerpieces consider using candles, fresh fruit and vegetables, outdoor items like pine cones, pine branches, leaves, flowering branches, sea shells or grape leaves. It's a good idea to avoid potted flowers for the table centerpiece since the dirt can sometimes contain small bugs.

For parties after dark, one of the most elegant and simple decorating ideas is to light candles everywhere. You can also line your front walkway or the edge of your backyard with inexpensive luminaria (small brown paper bags containing about an inch of sand in the bottom and a lit votive candle). If you have them, torches can add a festive look to your yard.

Another easy decorating tip is to pull out your tiny white Christmas lights from their storage boxes. They can be used around doorways, strung amidst your flowerbeds, or used for twinkling lights in trees and bushes.

General Party Tips

Music is an important part of any party since it helps to set the mood. It's important to remember to keep any music fairly quiet since you don't want people yelling to be heard—unless it's dance music rather than background mood music.

When parking your personal car, find a spot away from the area where guests will be parking. You don't want to get blocked by other cars in case you need to run to the store.

As you're preparing before the party, carry a timer in your pocket to remind you when to baste or stir food items.

Remember to be a good host/hostess: greet your guests, make sure someone takes their coats or shows them where to put their things, introduce your guests to each other and give them an idea of something they have in common as a conversation starter.

Simple Party Recipes

Spinach Dip:
1 package frozen spinach (thawed and drained), 16-

oz. sour cream, 1 can water chestnuts (chopped) and 1 package buttermilk ranch dressing mix. Mix together; chill. Serve inside large hollowed out sourdough bread round. Serve with chips, veggies.

Sweet Fruit Dip:

1 small container marshmallow cream, 8-oz. cream cheese. Blend together thoroughly. Serve cut up fruit with toothpicks for dipping: cantaloupe, honeydew, any melon, apples (red and green), bananas, grapes.

Easy Fruit Salad:

Cut up cantaloupe, honeydew, apples, bananas, grapes, any melon, raisins, nuts (walnuts, almonds or pecans). Stir in two small containers of Vanilla-flavored yogurt (not plain yogurt). Serve cold.

Have fun! If you've planned ahead carefully and done much of your party preparations in advance, you'll save money by not being surprised by last minute hidden expenses which tend to accumulate quickly without a definite plan detailed ahead of time.

Careful preparation will also allow you, as the host or hostess, to relax and enjoy your get-together as much as your friends and family.

Have a wonderful time!

5

CELEBRATING VALENTINE'S DAY ON A SHOESTRING BUDGET

Every year, whether we're ready for it or not, Valentine's Day comes around again. In case you've forgotten, it's always celebrated on February 14th. Now you have no excuse for ignoring it again this year.

But if you're thinking, "Well, I have no excuse except for the fact that I don't have much money to spend on an elaborate gift or dinner out at a fancy restaurant right now." No worries.

Here's a list of inexpensive—and often free—ideas for spending some quality romantic time with your Valentine.

Outdoor Ideas

If the weather outside isn't frightful this time of year where you live, Nature's always a romantic spot to spend some snuggling time together.

You could plan an exercise date if you're both fitness nuts: a brisk walk on a tree-lined lane, a game of Frisbee in the park with your favorite view, bicycling along the waterfront, a hike to a local destination. One of my favorite things to do is rent a canoe and meander slowly around the local waterways.

For a less physically demanding outdoor idea, slow the pace down and stroll leisurely through the park rather than power-walking. Hold hands, look at the flowers, watch the birds, listen to the sounds of nature. Go somewhere you haven't been for ages, maybe an arboretum, beach, game reserve, or Japanese gardens.

And don't let a bit of rainy drizzle stop your plans. A romantic stroll under a shared umbrella followed by a cup of coffee or tea in a local coffee shop is definitely a romantic alternative to the typically more expensive dinner and a movie. Plus, most parks are less crowded on rainy days, so you'll have more privacy for your romantic walk.

Even in the winter, it can be fun to wander through the local zoo. Many times the animals are more active this time of year rather than in the summer when they're all hiding in the shade, escaping the summer heat.

The local newspaper is always a great resource for

inexpensive date ideas. Check out the "What's Happening" section for information on local heritage festivals, film showings, street fairs, home tours, fireworks displays, musical events, and county fairs.

Indoor Activities

If it's too cold or wet to spend Valentine's Day outside, try taking a romantic drive together into the countryside, perhaps stopping for coffee and pie at a diner along the way. Mmm. Yummy!

Spend the afternoon browsing through antique stores together. Talk about the things you remember seeing in your grandmother's house when you were a child. It's amazing the memories that can come back looking through things from long ago. You might discover things about your loved one you never knew.

Museums are often a fairly inexpensive way to spend time together. Check around for history and art museums you've overlooked in the past. Many of them have free days, too.

If it's winter in your area and winter consists of sunny skies and palm trees, you might want to consider going ice skating together at the local skating rink. The change in temperature is invigorating, and it's fun to bundle up in a scarf and gloves if it's not something you do very often. Plus, it's always appropriate to hold hands while skating together. Instant romance!

Stay-at-Home Ideas

Breakfast in bed is a fun wake-up on Valentine's Day morning. Maybe cook some heart-shaped pancakes to complete the theme?

You could also have a tea party, just for the two of you with a selection of delicious gourmet teas, a variety of cakes and cookies, romantic music, and of course some fragrant flowers (they can just be ones picked from the yard. You don't have to go overboard—and over-budget—with a dozen long stemmed roses).

Try having a picnic in the living room by the fireplace. Spread a blanket or tablecloth on the floor, light some candles, pack traditional picnic food items into your picnic basket, turn on some soft music. Maybe feed each other fresh strawberries.

If you have a series of movies you both enjoy, a movie marathon can be a fun way to spend the day. Stock up on snacks ahead of time, cuddle under a blanket on the couch, and watch a day full of Lord of the Rings, the Matrix, or a variety of romantic comedies. Turn off the ringer on your phone and just spend the day getting lost in the stories together.

Have a happy Valentine's Day!

6

FRUGAL EASTER BASKET IDEAS

If you look forward to giving Easter baskets to your children each year but don't enjoy the high price of expensive pre-made baskets, here are some simple ideas for saving money on this fun holiday tradition. Like anything else you buy, it helps to set a spending limit— maybe $5 per Easter basket. Then have fun being creative and trying to keep within your basket budget.

When our kids were growing up, our family usually reserved Easter baskets and Easter Egg Hunts for the Saturday just before Easter, saving Sunday for church and family celebrations.

I always tried to shop for Easter basket fillers in advance (I used the same principle for Christmas stocking stuffers, too). You can keep a basket in the corner of a closet for storing these types of items found throughout the year. Keep an eye out for small games and toys in clearance bins at the grocery store, at dollar stores, and during any stops to thrift stores or yard sales.

In the days immediately following Halloween, bags of candy often go on sale for half price (or less), so I sometimes purchased several bags of family favorites and stuck them in the freezer. Frozen candy keeps quite nicely until Easter.

Small, fun items that you'll probably need to purchase for your children during the course of the year can be saved to include in their Easter baskets: crayons, felt pens, glue stick, glitter glue, novelty toothbrushes, fun-flavored toothpastes, hair ribbons, barrettes, a new hair brush, bubble bath in fun containers.

Ideas for the Basket, Itself

- Wicker baskets can be reused year after year (a nice tradition in itself). These can be used other times during the year for decoration or for storing small items. You can also reuse the decorative grass from year to year.

- Paper bags decorated with bunnies, eggs, flowers, etc.

- Easter bonnets. If you're going to be purchasing an Easter bonnet for your daughter, turn it upside down and fill with goodies.

- Inexpensive colorful plastic sand pails. Include a shovel and sand mold.

- Plastic mesh storage containers. Reuse to store toys, games, socks, childhood treasures, etc. Lunch box.

- New novelty pillowcase.

- Flower pot (fill w/packet of seeds, soil, drainage rocks, gardening gloves, instructions for growing their own Spring flowers).

- For older kids/teens, try a make-up container (including sample sizes of soap, perfume, lip gloss, nail polish, etc.), a fishing tackle box (include a few lures), a personal popcorn bowl (containing a bag of gourmet popcorn), or a new purse.

- For teen-agers or grown children, try a grocery bag filled with their favorite foods.

Basket Filling Ideas

Plastic eggs can be reused every year. Fill with jelly beans or small plastic toys of interest to the child. Bags full of fake bugs, dinosaurs, etc., can often be found at dollar stores for under a $1 per bag.

Other ideas include:

- Homemade candy and treats.
- Homemade frosted Easter-shaped cookies individually wrapped. You can also make cookie lollipops by adding a lollipop or ice cream stick before baking.
- Crispy Rice Treats or Popcorn Balls colored with pastel food coloring and shaped like eggs.
- Sidewalk Chalk Eggs: Mix 1 cup plaster, 1/2 cup water and several drops food coloring. Pour mixture into empty egg carton sections. When dry, peel away the carton and hot glue two sections together at the center to form a complete egg.
- Toys from fast food children's meals can be found in "like new" condition at thrift stores and yard sales for $0.25 or less.
- Rubber stamps and stamp pads.
- Homemade play dough.
- Crayons.
- Small bag of potato chips.
- Bubbles.
- A jump rope.
- Jacks.

- A Frisbee™.
- Chopsticks.
- Fancy shoelaces.
- Stickers.
- Books.
- Stationary, note cards, envelopes, stamps.
- Coloring books or coloring sheets. Find some simple Easter related clip-art and print the picture out in black and white for homemade coloring sheets, or print out several and staple them together for a custom made coloring book.
- Audio tapes you've made of yourself reading their favorite books aloud. Be sure to include a signal for them to turn the page if they'll be reading along with you.
- Look for small Dover Books at your local bookstore. These books are high quality and usually under $1 each. They have paper dolls, holiday activity books, coloring books, etc.

7

TEACHER APPRECIATION IDEAS

As the years go by, it seems to become more and common for parents to be expected to give gifts to their children's teachers at school. There's a fine line between showing appreciation and going broke. Finding just the right gift—at just the right price—can be challenging at best. And besides, how many apple-decorated key chains or coffee mugs can one teacher use?

Gina D., mother of four, says, "Every teacher appreciates school supplies. Often teachers spend a lot of their own money stocking their classrooms. I collect pencils, paper, whatever I can get inexpensively or in volume. I bought a big cube of construction paper for our use at home and sent half to my son's class. Last year, we made decorated glass ball ornaments by pouring several colors of acrylic paint into them and swirling the balls around to look marbled. It cost less than $2 per gift."

During the winter holiday season, teachers can be so busy with school-related holiday preparations that they don't have time or energy for all the necessary preparations at home. Home-baked cookies, etc., can be very helpful in this regard. Check for your school district's policy on homemade goodies, first, however.

The following are suggestions for helpful and often inexpensive teacher appreciation gifts for the holidays or the end of the school year:

- Shoebox-sized plastic storage box full of school and classroom supplies that you can stock up on throughout the year at sales, clearance stores, etc.
- Bag of popcorn and a flavored salt sampler.
- Gift certificate for a video rental.
- Homemade fudge in take-out meal containers (or Biscotti or gingerbread men).
- Pencils printed with their names on them.
- Painted glass ball ornaments.
- Flavored coffee or tea mixes.
- Coffee and cup decorated by your child.
- A candle and candleholder.
- Anything for the classroom: games, writing equipment, books, rulers, things to decorate or theme objects.
- Handmade items from the students (potholder,

pencil holder, etc.).

- Movie theater passes.
- Small basket of lotions or soaps.
- Letter or card from the student (and/or parent) telling what they enjoyed about the year or the teacher's input into the child's life.
- Small plant potted in a thrift store coffee mug or tea cup.
- Child-made apple-shaped something or other (although over the years many teachers end up with more apple decorations than they have room for in their house).
- Baked goods (bread, cookies, candies, quick breads, etc.).
- Chocolate dipped pretzels.
- Chocolate anything.
- Holiday ornament.

One woman online writes, "There are too many people who get left out and probably feel bad about it, such as the P.E. teacher, the principal, the secretary, the kitchen lady who knows your child by name, the teacher's aide who listens to them say their numbers or helps with reading, etc. And then there's the AWANA leader, the Girl/Boy Scout leader, the Sunday School teacher, and the private teachers like piano and dance. A parent can't possibly buy/make gifts for all these people."

Her unique suggestion to deal with this large number of potential gift recipients? Donate a book to the school or the public library "in the names of all the people who have been part of your child's life this year. Then give a card to each individual telling them why they were so important to your child and how this gift will help other children as much as he/she helped your child."

It's been my experience that people in volunteer helping positions (such as Sunday School teachers or nursery workers at church) are often completely overlooked when it comes time to give out thanks. Each year my husband and I try to invite our children's Sunday School teachers and their families to dinner at our house to thank them for all their hard work and dedication throughout the year.

It's never ceased to amaze me that I always hear comments like, "No one has ever done anything like this for me before and I've been teaching Sunday School for twelve years." Even just a simple Thank You card given at the holidays or the end of the school term could be enough to bowl them over in shock.

Remember, this isn't a competition to see which child or parent gives the teacher the best or most expensive gift. Showing appreciation to assorted teachers should be an expression of heartfelt thanks to the dedicated people who have touched our lives and given of themselves to our children.

8

SUCCESSFUL NEW YEAR'S RESOLUTIONS

The key to successfully implementing permanent change in our lives revolves around instituting new habits, and once a habit is made, we don't even have to think about it anymore.

I've found that the key to instilling new habits is choosing one habit—and only one—we want to work on at a time, and then focusing on that single habit for about four to six weeks, the amount of time it usually takes for a new behavior to become habitual.

After that first habit's been formed, we can then choose another habit to work on for a month or so, etc., etc.

A number of years ago I tried implementing a new health regiment for my New Year's resolution. The program I tried required life changes in the following areas:

- the amount of food I was eating
- what I ate
- how frequently I ate
- the amount of water I drank
- aerobic exercise
- using weights for strength training and body sculpting

All in all, I believe it was an excellent program ... but for someone like me who had allowed herself to fall so badly out of shape and away from healthy habits, attempting to overhaul every area of my eating/exercising life in one swoop was really a guaranteed failure before it began. Once again, I'd made another of those broken New Year's resolutions.

But what if instead of trying to change everything at once, I'd picked one idea at a time to work on until that one activity became habitual?

I could've started with one small step such as drinking enough water every day. Then the next month maybe I could've focused on aerobic walking three times per week. Or eating properly balanced meals. And then the next month focused on the timing of my meals.

In six months, I would've been able to simply and easily instill all six of the life changes from that program into my life without ever feeling overwhelmed by trying to do too much all at once. Instead of looking at my assorted food/exercise/health issues and feeling like a failure, I could've been making small and steady steps in the right direction each month and come out successfully at the other end.

One Habit at a Time

Okay, so we've all been told it takes four to six weeks for any action to become a habit. So, keeping that in mind, one way to insure success at keeping future New Year's resolutions is by working on only one new habit at a time each month. Then, every time you turn to a new calendar page, you can choose to work on developing a different good habit. At the end of the year, you could easily have twelve new positive habits in your life! Once something's become a habit, it's simply a part of life.

So, what's the area of life you're most concerned about this year? Exercise? Weight loss? Healthy eating? Getting organized? Saving money? Spending more time with your kids?

Whatever your area of focus might be, start by breaking your goal down into simple steps that you can easily manage. Then start working your way to your goal, one small step (or one small habit) at a time. As the old cliche' says: "How do you eat an elephant? One bite at a time." By making small and consistent changes, it's possible to change your health, your body, and your life.

My personal goals don't include becoming super-model thin or running a marathon. I want a healthy, balanced lifestyle rather than an obsessive diet/exercise regime that's based solely on quick results and what I want to see in the mirror. The mirror isn't my gauge of success. The energy and stamina and good health that comes for a balanced lifestyle is the success I want to see in my own life.

So, what about you? What single small step can you take this month toward a healthier New Year and a healthier new you? Choose one habit at a time. Take one step at a time. And before we know it, we'll all be where we want to be, not just healthy, but health-"wise."

9

FRIENDSHIP BAGS

A number of years ago, a young couple from our local church was pondering what to do about the various people they saw on street corners around town asking for food or money.

This couple didn't want to just hand out money. They weren't sure cash was going to be used in what they considered an appropriate manner, but they also didn't want to ignore sincere pleas for help from those truly in need.

After thinking about it, this couple came up with a simple idea that not only met the immediate needs of the person on the street corner, but also met the desire of the couple to provide help in a practical way without feeling someone might be taking advantage of their kind hearts.

Their solution? A great little idea they dubbed

"Friendship Bags." They made up several small paper lunch bags of inexpensive and helpful items (easy-open cans of food, juice, change for a phone call, etc.). They carried the bags with them in their car for those moments when someone waved a "Homeless. Need money for food!" sign next to their car window.

Eventually word got around to the leadership of the church about this couple's "Friendship Bags" and a new church ministry was born. Now every month, a small group of dedicated volunteers get together and make up a batch (about fifty) of Friendship Bags. These bags are then brought to the church and left in the foyer for anyone who'd like to keep a bag or two in their car for giving out as they're driving around town.

Each of the church's Friendship Bags contain:

- a pop-top can of fruit, or fruit cocktail
- a pop-top can of Vienna sausage
- a small can of juice
- a package of cheese and crackers, or peanut
- butter and crackers
- a napkin and plastic fork
- a moist towel-ette
- one all-day bus pass
- change for a local phone call
- a coupon for a free shower at the local YMCA
- a list of community contact phone numbers (crisis clinic, food bank, Salvation Army, etc.)

- a small tract or note from the church inviting them to stop by or call if they need any further assistance

If you've been puzzled about finding an appropriate response to the needy on our streets, perhaps making up a few Friendship Bags of your own might provide an answer. I find it makes for a great family project, too.

10

FAMILY ENTERTAINMENT ON A BUDGET

Being frugal doesn't mean you can't ever have any fun with your family. Sometimes it just takes a little creativity to find simple and inexpensive activities for all to enjoy.

- Be patient and wait to see new movies on video. Some communities even offer free video rentals at local libraries and will order new movies if library patrons request a certain title.

- Check to see if there are any discount movie theaters in your area. Most of these places show movies just before they're released to video. A family of four can go out for an evening at the movies and only spend around $10 for a fun family outing. Keep a list of movies you want to see, and then check the discount theater listings each week. These theaters often keep the movies for just one or two weeks, so stay alert to what's playing.

- Go to the first show of the day at first-run theaters for the best prices (and shortest lines!).

- Check your area for free days at museums, zoos, etc.

- Rather than buying separate admissions to different educational or fun family destinations, buy one yearly family pass to either the zoo, the aquarium, or a theme park. Go repeatedly to that one place each time you want a family outing. You will easily save the cost of the family admission, plus you'll have the benefit of not feeling pressured to see everything in one day. You can always see what you missed the next time you come. Next year, buy a pass somewhere else.

- Check for free concerts, plays, and other live family entertainment in local parks.

- Call and find out if your local college stage production group, ballet or orchestra will let you watch them rehearse for free.

- If you want to eat at an expensive restaurant, go for lunch rather than dinner. The menu is usually the same, but the prices are often half.

- When dining out, drink water only. Ask for a lemon or lime wedge if you want to make your drink seem special. This trick can easily cut $10 off your family's total dining bill, which could mean the difference between going out for a fun meal or staying home eating frozen egg rolls again.

- Go fly a kite. Literally!

- Make the most of any available student discounts. Show your child's school ID at museums, zoos, galleries, theaters, etc.

- Instead of an expensive day of professional sports, go to a high school or community college game.

11

FRUGAL FAMILY FIELD TRIP IDEAS

Family field trips are a simple, fun and fairly inexpensive educational enrichment activity you can enjoy regularly with your children.

- Many manufacturing plants offer free tours to families or small groups, and any free samples given out make great souvenirs when on vacation. Call ahead to find out about tour availability.

- Field trips to local attractions such as zoos or aquariums can be expensive, but purchasing an annual family pass pays for itself in just a couple trips. Knowing you can come back again and again, frees your family to thoroughly enjoy themselves without feeling the need to hurry and see everything in one day to get your money's worth out of the admission price. Return to the same site whenever you want a family outing, and then buy a pass to a different educational attraction next year.

- If your family enjoys attending live performances, check for free concerts, plays and other cultural events in local parks during the summer months.

- You can also contact college or community performance groups (drama, ballet, orchestra, etc.) to see if they'll allow you to watch them rehearse for free.

- Many local theater groups need volunteer ushers for their live performances. Volunteering in this manner is an excellent way for the older members of your family to gain free admission to a wide variety of cultural events, plus it provides a useful service to the local arts community.

12

200+ SUMMERTIME BOREDOM BUSTERS

Since we always tried not to use the phrase "I'm bored!" in our home, we usually didn't hear our kids complaining about being bored during those long days at home during the summer months.

But I have to admit that we were still an incredibly normal family. Even without the "b-word" in their vocabulary, there were still those times when my three children just seemed to be at a total loss for something constructive to do.

On one of those "I-can't-think-of-anything-to-do" days, I had my children sit down and make a list of everything they could do completely on their own without parental help. After they brainstormed about it for over an hour (which was a good anti-boredom activity itself), the kids had a list of about fifty activities. Surprisingly, they even included a few household chores like dusting and weeding!

I decided to ask for input from some other moms, and now my children have a list of over two hundred ideas to beat summertime boredom, and the list just kept growing.

Thanks to the suggestion of one mom, we put each item on this list onto individual pieces of paper, placed the papers into a container, and when the children needed inspiration for an activity, they would draw out two or three papers, and then decide which idea they wanted to do, either as a group or individually. The mom who suggested pulling ideas out of a container told me she found this method more helpful than giving the kids a huge list of possibilities. By narrowing the choices down to just two or three, it was easier for the kids to pick out the one that sounded the best or most interesting to them.

200+ Ideas for Summertime Activities

In no particular order, here's our current (but continually growing!) list of activities:

1. ride bikes
2. roller blade
3. basketball
4. play board games
5. make a tent out of blankets

6. squirt with hoses
7. run through the sprinkler
8. jump rope
9. read books
10. blow bubbles
11. make homemade play dough
12. play with play dough
13. press flowers
14. do crafts with pressed flowers
15. write a letter to a relative, friend or pen pal
16. clean bedroom
17. vacuum living room
18. clean bathroom
19. make a craft
20. draw
21. color
22. paint
23. pull weeds
24. watch a movie
25. write stories
26. use binoculars
27. use magnifying glass
28. use microscope
29. bird watching
30. write a play
31. act out a play
32. invent circus acts
33. perform a circus
34. play card games
35. make art on the front walkway with sidewalk

THE SIMPLE MOM'S IDEA BOOK

chalk
36. play catch
37. play baseball
38. collect rocks
39. collect leaves
40. collect feathers
41. play Frisbee
42. make Frisbee's out of old plastic lids, decorate with markers
43. dust the house
44. brush the pet
45. write letters
46. read a magazine
47. play dress-up
48. play Cowboys
49. pick vegetables
50. play outside with the pet
51. build a fort in your rooms
52. build a fort in the backyard
53. do a jigsaw puzzle
54. play on the Geo-Safari or other educational game
55. play on the computer
56. listen to a story or book on tape
57. do extra schoolwork to get ahead
58. do brain teasers (ie: crosswords, word searches, hidden pictures, mazes, etc.)
59. cook
60. prepare lunch
61. surprise a neighbor with a good deed
62. play store

63. prepare a "restaurant" lunch with menus
64. hold a tea party
65. have a Teddy bear picnic
66. play with toy cars
67. play dolls
68. play house
69. chase butterflies
70. collect caterpillars and bugs
71. plant a garden or a pot
72. collect seeds
73. hunt for four-leaf clovers
74. learn magic tricks
75. put on a magic show
76. plant a container garden
77. sprout seeds or beans
78. make sock puppets
79. put on a puppet show
80. make Christmas presents
81. make homemade wrapping paper
82. make homemade gift cards
83. make picture frames from twigs glued onto sturdy cardboard
84. crochet or knit
85. make doll clothes
86. sew buttons in designs on old shirts
87. run relay races
88. make bookmarks
89. take a quiet rest time
90. take a shower or bath
91. bathe a pet

92. feed the birds or squirrels
93. watch the clouds
94. organize a dresser drawer
95. clean under the bed
96. empty dishwasher
97. vacuum under the couch cushions and keep any change found
98. write these ideas on pieces of paper and pick out one or two to do
99. whittle
100. whittle bars of soap
101. practice musical instruments
102. perform a family concert
103. teach yourself to play musical instrument (recorder, harmonica, guitar)
104. fold laundry
105. sweep kitchen or bathroom floors
106. sweep front walkway
107. sweep or spray back patio
108. sweep or spray driveway
109. wash car
110. vacuum car
111. vacuum or dust window blinds
112. clean bathroom mirrors
113. clean sliding glass doors
114. clean inside of car windows
115. wash bicycles
116. clean garage
117. play in the sandbox
118. build a sandcastle

119. work with clay
120. copy your favorite book illustration
121. design your own game
122. build with blocks or Legos
123. create a design box (copper wire, string, odds-and-ends of things destined for the garbage, pom-poms, thread, yarn, etc.)
124. plan a neighborhood or family Olympics
125. have a marble tournament
126. paint a picture with lemon juice on white paper and hang it in a sunny window and see what happens in a few days
127. finger paint with pudding
128. make dessert
129. make dinner
130. give your pet a party
131. paint the sidewalk with water
132. start a journal of summer fun
133. start a nature diary
134. have a read-a-thon with a friend or sibling
135. have a neighborhood bike wash
136. play flashlight tag
137. play Kick the Can
138. check out a science book and try some experiments
139. make up a story
140. arrange photo albums
141. find bugs and start a collection
142. do some stargazing
143. decorate bikes or wagons and have a

neighborhood parade

144. catch butterflies and then let them go
145. play hide-and-seek
146. create a symphony with bottles and pans and rubber bands
147. listen to the birds sing
148. try to imitate bird calls
149. read a story to a younger child
150. find shapes in the clouds
151. string dry noodles or O-shaped cereals into a necklace
152. glue noodles into a design on paper
153. play hopscotch
154. play jacks
155. make up a song
156. make a teepee out of blankets
157. write in your journal
158. find an ant colony and spill some food and watch what happens
159. play charades
160. make up a story by drawing pictures
161. draw a cartoon strip
162. make a map of your bedroom, house or neighborhood
163. call a friend
164. cut pictures from old magazines and write a story
165. make a collage using pictures cut from old magazines
166. do a secret service for a neighbor

167. plan a treasure hunt
168. make a treasure map
169. make up a "Bored List" of things to do
170. plan a special activity for your family
171. search your house for items made in other countries and then learn about those countries from the encyclopedia or online
172. plan an imaginary trip to the moon
173. plan an imaginary trip around the world, where would you want to go
174. write a science-fiction story
175. find a new pen pal
176. make up a play using old clothes as costumes
177. make up a game for practicing math facts
178. have a Spelling Bee
179. make up a game for practicing spelling
180. surprise an elderly or homebound neighbor or relative by weeding his/her garden
181. finger paint with shaving cream
182. collect sticks and mud and build a bird's nest
183. write newspaper articles for a pretend newspaper
184. put together a family newsletter
185. write reviews of movies or plays or TV shows or concerts you see during the summer
186. bake a cake
187. bake a batch of cookies
188. decorate a shoe box to hold your summer treasures
189. make a hideout or clubhouse

190. make paper airplanes
191. have paper airplane races
192. learn origami
193. make an obstacle course in your backyard
194. make friendship bracelets for your friends
195. make a wind chime out of things headed for the garbage
196. paint your face
197. braid hair
198. play tag
199. make a sundial
200. make food sculptures (from pretzels, gumdrops, string licorice, raisins, cream cheese, peanuts, peanut butter, etc.) and then eat it
201. make a terrarium
202. start a club
203. take a nap outside on your lawn
204. produce a talent show
205. memorize a poem
206. recite a memorized poem for your family.

13

EMERGENCY KITCHEN SUBSTITUTIONS

Do you ever find yourself all geared up and ready to make a favorite recipe, but then discover you're staring at an empty container of a needed ingredient? Ugh. You don't want to run out to the store right now. So what do you do?

Well, that's when Emergency Kitchen Substitutions come in handy. I've printed out the following list and keep a copy taped to the inside of my pantry door at all times.

Although these recipe ingredient substitutions will work in a pinch, I don't recommend always substituting ingredients in your recipes. The recipes will technically work with substitutions, but often the finished product won't be exactly the same as when you use the original ingredients called for in the recipe.

Also, be sure you don't make more than one substitution in a particular recipe at once. The more ingredients you substitute, the more "off" your product will be when you're finished.

Emergency Substitutions

- For: 1 Tbsp. fresh herb
  Use: 1/3 to 1/2 tsp. dried herb (of the same kind)

- For: 1 clove garlic
  Use: 1/8 tsp. garlic powder

- For: 1 egg in baking
  Use: 1 tsp. cornstarch plus 1/4 cup water

- For: 1 whole egg
  Use: 2 egg yolks plus 1 Tbsp. water

- For: 1 cup whole fresh milk
  Use: 1/2 cup evaporated milk plus 1/2 cup water, or 1/3 cup dry milk plus 1 cup water

- For: 1 cup buttermilk
  Use: 1 cup plain yogurt or 1 cup sour milk (4 tsp. White vinegar or lemon juice plus milk to make 1 cup—let it sit for five minutes before using)

- For: 1 cup sour cream (in baking)
  Use: 7/8 cup buttermilk or sour milk plus 3 Tbsp. of butter

- For: 1 cup sour cream (in salad dressings, casseroles)
  Use: 1 cup plain yogurt or 3/4 cup sour milk plus 1/3 cup butter

- For: 1 cup cream
  Use: 1/3 cup butter plus 3/4 cup milk

- For: 1 cup corn syrup
  Use: 2/3 cup granulated sugar plus 1/3 cup water

- For: 1 cup brown sugar
  Use: 1 cup granulated sugar plus 2 Tbsp. molasses

- For: 1 3/4 cup Confectioner's sugar
  Use: 1 cup granulated sugar, packed

- For: 1 cup margarine or butter (in baking or cooking)
  Use: 1 cup hard shortening or 7/8 cup vegetable oil

- For: 1 square unsweetened chocolate
  Use: 3 Tbsp. cocoa plus 1 Tbsp. oil

- For: 1 ounce semi-sweet chocolate
  Use: 1 ounce unsweetened chocolate plus 4 tsp. sugar

- For: 3/4 cup cracker crumbs
  Use: 1 cup bread crumbs

- For: 1 cup cake flour, sifted
  Use: 7/8 cup all-purpose flour, sifted (1 cup minus 2 Tbsp.)

- For: 1 tsp. baking powder
  Use: 1/3 tsp. baking soda plus 1/2 tsp. cream of tartar, or 1/4 tsp. baking soda plus 1/3 cup sour milk

- For: 1 Tbsp. cornstarch for thickening
  Use: 2 Tbsp. flour

- For: 1 Tbsp. flour for thickening
  Use: 1 1/2 tsp. corn flour, arrowroot, potato flour, or rice flour; or 2 tsp. tapioca

- For: 2 Tbsp. tapioca for thickening
  Use: 3 Tbsp. flour

14

LET'S PLAY "HIDE-AND-SNEAK" WITH VEGETABLES

Do you find yourself sitting by helplessly while your very own little picky eater works her way through every ounce of spaghetti sauce, picking out the almost microscopic bits of cooked onion?

Do you wish there were a way to get little Johnny to eat more veggies than just the French fries at the local drive-thru? (Do those even count as veggies?)

Well, relax.

While the following tricks won't necessarily help you win each of those out-right battles waged over plates of food with flagrant veggies and fruit, playing a little "Hide-and-Sneak" could be just what the doctor ordered for a simple way to help your child eat healthier ... even if their picky little taste buds haven't quite matured enough for a full serving of cooked Brussel sprouts.

1. Puree veggies and add to spaghetti sauce, soups, or soup stock. You can also use small baby food jars of pureed carrots or squash to thicken (and add some healthy veggies) to assorted sauces and soups.

2. Shred veggies and add to ground meat for healthier burgers, meatloaf, or meatballs. You can also add some shredded veggies as you're browning ground meat for tacos and other ground meat meals.

3. Hide those "icky" onions in sauces, casseroles, or other recipes by sauteing the sliced onions in a small amount of margarine/butter or olive oil until soft. Then blending thoroughly in the blender. You'll get all of the delicious onion flavor but none of that yucky "slimy" texture picky kids tend to find so disgusting.

4. Thicken gravies and sauces with pureed vegetables (be sure to steam or cook the veggies first). You can also use baby food veggies for this, too

5. Add 1/2 cup of carrot puree (or a jar of those handy baby food carrots) to your favorite brownie

mix or chocolate cake recipe.

6. Let your kids "dip" their various raw or cooked veggies in a dip: Cheese dip, Ranch dressing, salsa, mayo, sour cream, or ketchup. One mom reported to me that her daughter's veggie-with-dip of choice is cooked green beans dipped in her favorite ketchup. Yeah, I know. Ick! But at least she's eating those green beans happily.

7. Make your own fruit-flavored breakfast "syrups" by blending fresh or thawed blueberries, strawberries, raspberries or whatever you child's favorite berries might be with a small amount of honey.

8. Make popsicles with 100% fruit juice, pureed fruit mixed with a bit of honey and juice or milk, or flavored yogurt.

Be creative. Invent your own version of "Hide-and-Sneak" with your picky child's personal food arch-enemy.

15

BUILDING A BETTER BURGER

One thing I often hear from guests is that my barbequed burgers actually taste good, rather than just being hard and dry as hockey pucks like so many of those traditional family reunion barbequed hamburgers we've all endured from time to time.

In honor of the hallowed summertime tradition of outdoor cooking, here are some of my favorite tips for finding your way to Hamburger Heaven in your own backyard.

1) Don't build your burger from low fat meat.

Get a package of ground beef with an 80/20 or even a 70/30 ratio of meat to fat. The fat keeps it moist and flavorful and drains off during the cooking process so the calorie count ultimately isn't much higher than the lower fat varieties ... but the flavor is so much better. Be aware, though, that the higher the fat content in your meat, the more the patty will shrink while cooking. So plan accordingly.

2) For additional flavor, try mixing ground beef with other ground meats like pork, sausage or lamb.

A good ratio is two parts beef to one part other meat. Also, if you use ground turkey to save money, keep in mind that turkey is probably one of the least stable burger materials you can find, so mix it 50/50 with ground beef to keep those burgers in one piece on the grill.

3) When forming burgers, mix the ingredients together gently.

Handle your burger patties as little as possible, and don't fully compress the meat ... remember, you're not making meatloaf or meatballs. If you form the raw beef into patties with wet hands, the grease won't stick to your skin nearly as much.

4) If you like adding extra things to your ground beef before making patties, make sure to keep the pieces small.

Large chunks of onion or garlic make the patty

unstable and more apt to fall apart while cooking. Be sure to finely chop or grate all added veggies.

5) Some particularly tasty additions to the burger mix are: freshly ground pepper, minced garlic, finely chopped onion, Worcestershire sauce, grated carrot, crushed vinegar and salt potato chips, or soy sauce.

I've discovered that burger purists tend to insist on top-of-the-line ground beef (Sirloin) with nothing added but salt and pepper (after grilling). Honestly, I love a good, pure burger ... but sometimes it's fun to add the extras for variety. Also, if you add steak sauce or applesauce to your burger patties, try mixing in some dry bread crumbs, quick-cooking oats, or beaten eggs to help stabilize the burgers.

6) Cook over a medium flame rather than a high one.

You want to cook the patties just slow enough to cook all the way through. You don't want them charred on the outside and a raw mess on the inside.

7) Don't press down on the cooking burger patties with your spatula or flip the burger using tongs that squeeze the burger.

You'll just be squeezing out all the delicious juiciness and leaving behind a much dryer and tougher finished product. Make an indentation with your thumb in the center of each burger before cooking to help keep them flat without squishing them under the spatula.

8) Never—I repeat, never!—poke your cooking burger patties with a fork or other pointy object.

It's a guaranteed trip to Hockey Puck Hamburger Land when all those delicious juices pour out through that hole.

9) The less you move the burgers around on the grill, the better looking the grill marks.

Ideally, you only want to turn the burger once, but be sure to focus on safety and full cooking more than making the prettiest burgers on the block. You'll hear mixed messages from burger aficionados about what temperature to cook the burgers and how often to flip them, but I tend to not worry about the perfect grill marks and have found that frequent flipping tends to keep the juices in the burger a bit better.

10) Let the burgers rest for a minute or two before serving to give a chance for the juices to settle.

Serving too soon may cause the burgers to dry out. Rather than melting cheese onto the burgers during the grilling process, I like to set the cheese slices on top of the finished burgers while they're "resting." The cheese melts without dripping off the burger onto the grill.

When the cheese is done melting, the burgers are done resting and ready to serve.

Add your favorite toppings and enjoy!

16

HEALTHY AND INEXPENSIVE MEAT SUBSTITUTE

What if I told you I'd found a food you can use like meat that's not only dirt cheap, but also healthier than many other food items on the market? You'd probably think I also had some swamp land in Florida to sell you cheap.

Well, TVP (texturized vegetable protein) is the "wonder" food in question. TVP is basically an inexpensive, relatively tasteless meat substitute which can be added to many dishes you're probably already fixing for your regular family meals. Not recommended for people with soy allergies or sensitivities, however.

TVP's texture is similar to that of ground meat, it's very low in fat and has no cholesterol. Since TVP is nearly tasteless, it absorbs the flavor of whatever you're cooking. I've found TVP tends to work best in fairly spicy dishes rather than bland recipes. We use TVP in spaghetti sauce, chili, soups, Sloppy Joes, skillet meals and tacos.

For skeptical family members, you can even try sneaking TVP into your recipes mixed half-and-half with ground beef or turkey. The first time I snuck it into spaghetti sauce, my family commented on how good the meal was, and no one suspected that the meat-like granules in the sauce weren't ground beef or sausage.

TVP comes in dry form (several different shapes/sizes: flakes, chunks, granules) and there are now also several flavored varieties. Since it comes dry, TVP needs to be reconstituted before using.

To reconstitute, simply pour one cup boiling water over one cup dry TVP, letting it sit in a bowl until the TVP absorbs all the water (this just takes a couple minutes). If I'm adding TVP to something with a high water content such as spaghetti sauce or soup, I don't bother rehydrating it first since it will absorb the flavorful liquid from the sauce/soup.

I purchase TVP in the bulk food bins at my local health food co-op, but I've also seen it carried in several major grocery store chains. Just call around and find the stores in your local area that carry it.

17

BEATING THE BREAKFAST RUSH HOUR

In many families, morning is a hectic and hurried time. Frequently parents feel fortunate just to get everyone out the door fully dressed each day. Serve a hot cooked breakfast every morning? Not a chance.

Breakfast (if it's served at all) often consists of grabbing a toaster pastry and a quick glass of juice as the family runs out the door racing headlong to work and school.

I've discovered that taking an hour or two on an occasional weekend to prepare breakfast items for the freezer, takes much of the insanity out of the weekday morning rush.

Waffles, Pancakes, French Toast

To prepare waffles, pancakes and French toast for freezing, cook until lightly browned. Don't overcook. Then freeze individually in a single layer on a cookie sheet or flat pan.

When frozen solid, stack together in a freezer bag. By freezing these items separately, they won't stick together. You can remove only the amount needed for today's meal whether it's one waffle or a dozen.

To reheat, just pop them (still frozen) into the toaster on the pastry setting (low) just like you would do with the boxed frozen waffles from the store.

Heating in a toaster keeps them firm, rather than limp and soggy which often happens when these breakfast items are reheated in the microwave.

Muffins and Quick Breads

Make muffins and quick breads ahead of time to serve for easy breakfasts. Just bake your favorite recipes as usual, cool completely, wrap in foil, label, and freeze.

You can also wrap individual muffins in plastic wrap and then place the wrapped muffins into large zip-top freezer bags. Muffins can be easily reheated in the microwave.

Serve with fresh fruit and juice for a delicious and easy breakfast.

18

THE JOYS OF CROCKERY COOKING

When I think of crockery cooking, I always see in my mind's eye, my mother's old avocado-green crock sitting on the turquoise and white kitchen counter. What a thing of a beauty it was … NOT!

But today's crockery cookers are sleek, modern appliances you don't have to hide away in the dark recesses of the pantry or garage anymore.

If you like the experience of walking in the door and smelling dinner cooking without you slaving away in the kitchen preparing the meal, you'll love the convenience of a crockery cooker.

Take a few minutes in the morning before work or school to throw some ingredients into the pot, set it and forget it. When you come home at dinnertime, you'll be greeted by the heavenly aroma of an easy dinner. What could be better than that?

At the end of the day when I'm tired and ready to put my feet up, the last thing I want to do is dive into a bunch of meal preparation work. But in the morning, I'm refreshed and able to put more energy into food prep. But even then, it's not much food prep. Maybe a bit of chopping and browning, but no more than ten or fifteen minutes worth of work, at the most.

The Benefits of Crockery Cooking

Some of the benefits you'll find from dusting off that lovely retro-crock in the back of Grandma's attic are:

- You can buy tougher (and less expensive) cuts of meat because the crock acts as a tenderizer
- Meat shrinks less when cooked in the crock, and doesn't dry out
- A crockery cooker doesn't heat up the kitchen nearly as much as the stovetop or oven, so it's a perfect hot weather cooking appliance
- Frees up space in oven and stove top, great to use for parties, large gatherings, or doing a large cooking session for the freezer
- Flavors have time to develop while your meal slowly cooks all day
- Tofu tastes better cooked this way because it has

time to soak up the flavors from broth, spices and other ingredients

- Can be used on a buffet table for serving hot foods (soup, stew, sauces, meatballs in barbeque sauce, etc.)

Crockery Cooker Tips

You'll want to keep the following tips in mind when choosing and using your crock:

- Choose a crock with a removable liner. You'll have more flexibility in ways to use it, and it's easier to clean.
- Buy a large one.
- Best if used for recipes with a high water content – things you'd normally prepare on the stovetop such as spaghetti, soup, chili, stew.
- For best results, fill the crock at least half full with food and/or liquid.
- If you're cooking something like a stew or soup, leave at least an inch (preferably two inches) empty at the top beneath the lid to allow for the food to bubble when it reaches a simmer.
- Don't peek! Lifting the lid adds time to the cooking process by letting heat out. Add 15-20 minutes to the cooking time for every time you lift the lid to peek or stir.

- High altitudes need longer cooking times. Check with your crock's Manufacturer's User's Guide for their recommendations.
- Brown meats ahead of time for additional color and flavor.
- Browning also removes some of the fat from the meat. Fatty meat cooks more quickly in the crock than lean meat.
- Meat and poultry cooks best if cut into smaller pieces or chunks rather than cooking as a whole roast or a whole chicken.
- Fish and seafood should be added near the end of the cooking time in seafood soups, stews and chowders.
- Vegetables such as carrots and potatoes, should be added to the bottom of the crock beneath any meats, etc. Hard vegetables need a longer cooking time, and the bottom is the first part of the cooker to heat up, so they'll start cooking sooner.
- Stir in cheese at the end of cooking, or use processed cheese.
- Milk curdles during long cooking times. Add milk near end of cooking time (the last hour, or so).
- Add spices near the end of the cooking time.
- Stirring usually isn't required during slow cooking on Low heat. You might want to stir once or twice during the last hour, but remember that every time you lift the lid, you're adding to the cooking time. Two stirring sessions equal a

minimum of half an hour longer cooking.

Suggestions for a Safe and Sane Crock

The crock itself should be safe to use providing you don't have an old one with frayed cords or some other defect. The following tips on safe user ideas can help keep your family healthy and the cook from being burned:

- Use fresh or completely thawed meats. Don't add frozen meats directly to the crock.
- Be sure the crock is clean before using.
- Keep perishable foods refrigerated until ready to use.
- Always include liquids in all crockery cooking recipes.
- Remove the cover by opening away from your face. The steam is hot enough to burn badly.
- Don't leave a slow cooker turned off with food in it for any length of time. Start cooking right away, and serve hot from the cooker.
- Don't let food sit at room temperature to cool.
- Keep the crock covered while cooking. The lid on a crock doesn't provide a tight seal (it isn't supposed to), but it's important to keep the lid in the center of the crock for best results.
- Don't set the hot crock on a cold surface unless you put a hot pad, trivet or towel underneath.

- If the power goes out while you're away from home with the crock running, throw the food away even if it looks hot and done. The power might have been off long enough for the food to cool, start growing bacteria, and then reheat by the time you arrived home.

- Don't reheat leftovers in a crock, but you can use the crock as a food warmer for foods that have been cooked and heated in the oven or on the stovetop.

19

AVOIDING MOSQUITO BITES

One of the best ways to keep mosquitoes from getting the bite on you is to avoid being the main attraction at your local mosquito theme park in the first place. Understanding a bit about mosquito behavior can help avoid calling unnecessary attention to yourself.

Mosquitoes identify their targets by sight, heat and smell. Avoid physically active movement (exercise, ball games, yard work, etc.) during peak mosquito hours to keep them from noticing you from a distance.

Peak mosquito times tend to be right around dusk and dawn. Reduce outside lights in the evening hours (use yellow bulbs, if possible).

Wear light colors during the daytime, as dark clothing during daylight hours actually attracts the little buggers. According to one report, mosquitoes prefer blue and green so you're better off wearing yellows, reds and oranges.

Mosquitoes are attracted to perspiration, heat, carbon dioxide, and lactic acid. All of these are produced after exercising, so avoid outdoor exercise during peak mosquito hours (at dawn and dusk). Our bodies also release lactic acid after eating certain foods, so avoiding outdoor dining during those hours is helpful, as well. Commonly believed mosquito-attracting foods include bananas (or other potassium-rich food items), and salty foods.

Avoid perfumes when outside. Using hand creams and lotions with a sweet scent can also increase your risk of attracting mosquitoes, so go for the unscented varieties during mosquito season. Try using unscented soaps when showering, too. Even though they're rinsed off, the scent remains on your skin and attracts bugs.

Keeping a barrier between yourself and mosquitoes is a simple and natural way to avoid bites. Be sure to wear long sleeves and long pants when outdoors at dusk, or in areas with an especially high concentration of mosquitoes (woods, swamps, hiking trails). And use screens in all your home's doors and windows during summer months.

Several gardeners assured me that planting marigolds, scented geraniums (rub the leaves on your skin too), rosemary, catnip, peppermint, spearmint, daisies, verbena, spike lavender (not the sweet French variety), basil, thyme, garlic, allspice, cedar, and lemon grass around the yard naturally repels insects. Decorating with eucalyptus is also rumored to be helpful. You can make your own insect-repelling sachets by drying the flowers and leaves from the above plants and placing them into small, hand-sewn cotton bags.

Eliminate Mosquito Breeding Grounds

The first step in avoiding the bite is to eliminate the local mosquito population at its source. Mosquitoes use stagnant water for their breeding grounds, so drain any collections of stagnant water found in your yard, neighborhood or workplace.

Keep your eye out for these sources of standing water:

- discarded tires
- roof gutters clogged with leaves or other debris
- rain barrels
- wading pools
- drainage ditches
- paint buckets
- tin cans
- paper cups or other discarded trash
- trash containers
- infrequently used yard equipment
- plant containers
- bird baths
- broken toys
- pet water bowls

- holes in tree stumps

If your kids want to play in their wading pool, be sure to dump the water out at least once a week and turn the pool upside down when not in use so rain doesn't collect in it.

And if you want to keep your birdbath and pet's outdoor watering bowl, be sure to clean out the water at least two times each week. If you have an outdoor fish pond with goldfish or amphibians, the fish will eat the mosquito larva so you won't need to drain the fish pond.

"Shoo Fly! Don't Bother Me!"

With the advent of mosquito season, many people feel concern for more than just the annoying itchiness of a bite or two. Worries about West Nile Virus and other mosquito-carried diseases have led many who would normally avoid excessive use of chemicals to start spraying and slathering on insect repellents containing the chemical DEET (N,N-diethyl-m-toluamide).

Safer Use of Chemical Repellents

If you feel you simply must spray yourself or your child with an insect repellent containing DEET, try to keep the repellent away from your child's face.

If you apply it to the face, spray or rub the repellent onto your hands first and then apply from your fingers to the face rather than spraying or applying directly from the bottle or tube to the skin. Insects often bite the lower extremities, so spraying or applying lotion to your legs and feet (especially if they're wearing sandals during the summer months) is particularly helpful.

Avoid using DEET-containing products on your child's hands because more often than not, their hands will eventually transfer the DEET to their mouth.

Don't spray or apply DEET products over cuts, scratches, rashes, or other open spots in the skin.

Natural Alternatives

But are there valid, healthier options when it comes to repelling our fine buzzing and biting friends? You bet! Some ideas for natural insect repellents fall into the category of folklore, myth and urban legends, but other natural remedies can be an effective means of protecting yourself and your loved ones from biting bugs and harsh chemicals.

Natural insect repellents tend to provide coverage for a shorter time, but their coverage is safer so you may find it worth the extra effort applying a bit more often.

Most natural repellents only offer about one-tenth of the protection time found in DEET-containing products, so plan on reapplying every 30 minutes or so. Because of their shorter protection time, natural repellents are ideal for short evening outdoor activities like walking the dog, barbecuing, or watering the garden.

Remember, don't spray or apply any insect repellents (natural or chemical) over cuts, scratches, rashes, or other open spots in the skin. Also, be sure to avoid the eye area when applying repellents.

Essential Oils as Natural Repellents

The most common, and most effective, natural insect repellents are various essential oils. Clove oil and citronella (rose geranium) are the most effective against mosquitoes, but be careful with clove oil and use it sparingly. It can be a skin irritant.

Other fairly effective essential oils include lemon grass, eucalyptus, castor oil, peppermint, tea tree oil, lavender, and cedar. You can buy cedar oil in spray-on bottles at your local pet store.

It's important to remember when using essential oils, don't use them internally! They need to be used externally on your skin and garments.

Be sure to test any oils on a small patch of skin before applying widely to your body to avoid allergic reactions or skin irritations.

You can make your own insect repellent sprays by combining rubbing alcohol (or witch hazel, vodka, or olive oil) with one of the listed essential oils (about 10-to-1, alcohol-to-oil ratio). Shake well before each use.

To make a lotion, use two ounces distilled water, two ounces olive oil, and about 120 drops essential oil. Put the water into a deep mixing bowl, and using a wire whip, begin beating quickly while slowly drizzling in the olive oil. After oil is mixed into the distilled water, stir in the essential oil of your choice (citronella is probably the most effective for insect repellent use).

You can also add a few drops of your choice of insect-repelling essential oils to your shampoo or liquid soap to help counteract the perfumes in these products.

Keep in mind that the following criteria reduces the effectiveness of all insect repellents: clothing rubbing on your skin, natural evaporation, your skin's natural ability to absorb anything applied to it, sweat or rain washing off the repellent, and a windy environment.

Some folks claim that garlic is an effective insect repellent, but I think it works best for repelling friends (or maybe a vampire or two).

20

STRIVING FOR BALANCE, ONE HABIT AT A TIME

The biggest thing that seemed to keep me from pursuing healthy eating habits for any significant length of time was personal time constraints. Busy, busy, busy. Like many people today, I didn't have time to get home-cooked meals on the table regularly—much less take the time to actually prepare something nutritious and healthy.

Then something happened several summers ago that completely changed my wishy-washy approach to healthful eating.

One morning I was showering and discovered what every woman dreads: a lump. A sizeable lump. Suddenly I was at the doctor's office having x-rays and ultrasounds done, and before I really had time to fathom the full repercussions of this new chapter in my life, I was being schedule for a surgical lumpectomy and biopsy.

The earliest they could schedule the procedure was several weeks away, so I found myself in "waiting mode," trying not to obsess about my health, but finding myself helplessly reevaluating everything in my life.

It seemed that in one swift, life-changing moment I'd gone from peacefully going about my quiet little life to suddenly examining every moment and activity in light of the question, "What if . . . ?" What if I have cancer? What if I get horribly sick? What if I die? What if I don't live to see my children grow up? What if this is my last summer here on Earth? What if …?

My entire life was now under a high-power microscope. I'd find myself looking at an activity and thinking, "Is this how I would want to spend my time if this were the last week of my life?" More often than not, the answer was a resounding, "No!"

Suddenly everything stood out like a relief map. It was easy to identify priorities in a way I never had before. And I'd lived for a long time with a clear set of priorities before me. But my priorities took on new meaning; I sensed a new urgency.

My children. My husband. My faith. These priorities suddenly grew in importance as my focus changed. Other activities like writing, public speaking, Internet activities and even mundane things like housework lessened their hold over my life. Not that those things ceased to be important but their placement in the way I chose to spend my time and energy changed.

But probably the biggest refocusing that occurred was in the area of my physical health. For many years I'd been eating a poor diet and living a sedentary lifestyle. And my poor body showed it. Out of shape, overweight, out of breath.

The Biopsy Results

The biopsy was negative. Really? Did the doctor's office actually say the results were negative—as in "no cancer"?

A moment of numbness and then: Hallelujah! That was truly a day for rejoicing when I heard those comforting test results.

My entire life had been on hold while I waited to have the surgical lumpectomy. I was happy (jubilant? ecstatic? outrageously euphoric?) about the tests results, but I had a fairly difficult recovery time. I didn't know it was possible to bruise so badly or hurt so much. As I waited out my body's healing process, I realized the non-physical scars from this event were going to last a lot longer than any physical ones. My emotional and spiritual life had received a jolt that would leave me forever changed.

I remember lying in the recovery room after the surgery promising myself that as soon as I was able, I would start physically working out and eating better. I had a strong new motivation.

My brush with the harsh realities of the brevity and uncertainty of life made me want more than anything else to do whatever it took to live a full and healthy life, to see my children grow up and hopefully my grandchildren too.

A Photo's Worth a Thousand Words

In addition to this new inner motivation, I knew I needed something concrete to be a constant reminder of just how out of shape I was and how badly I needed to follow through on this health program.

Enter the idea of taking a "before" photo. Oh my goodness. Can you say, "Scary"?

I dressed myself in my then several-sizes-too-small swimsuit and had my daughter take photographs of me from every angle. There's no hiding the truth from the camera. When those pictures came back from the photo developer (and no, I didn't go to the store to pick them up personally!), I cringed when I saw them. Cringe is a drastic understatement. I flinched. I winced. I cowered. I maybe even shed a tear or two.

Seeing my own bare back was an eye-opening event for me. My back is that part I just don't see—actually I can't see it without a photograph or doing the contortions of a gymnast in front of a full-length mirror.

I gazed at those photos, dumbfounded. What had happened to me? When did I develop the widest back West of the Mississippi? I can remember being an adult and wearing a size 5 pair of slacks. But not today. Maybe I could get one leg into a size 5 now!

I looked at those pictures and thought, "Whatever happened to that thin young thing I used to be? When was my body taken over by an Alien Cow?"

Well, three babies and many years of a sedentary lifestyle and poor food choices had taken a toll on my poor body.

Over the years, it had been easy to look in the mirror, put on my make-up, and think I didn't look too bad if I was having a good hair day, but then never *really* look at myself or take an honest inventory of my health.

Those photos were the most horrifying thing I've ever seen. No wonder I was always the first person to offer to take group photos so I wouldn't have to actually be in any of the pictures myself. I think I was trying to hide the truth about what was happening to my body from myself.

Realistic Goals

I want to be healthy and strong and I'm honestly less interested in how I look than how I feel. But seeing my physical self as I really looked to others was just the wake-up call I needed.

So whenever I'm tempted to have second helpings, or just one more handful of potato chips, or devour a full box of cookies, I take out those pictures of my back and look at them closely. I quickly lose my appetite for junk and find myself reaching for a piece of fresh fruit or slice of low-fat cheese instead.

For me, the journey to a healthier lifestyle began with two steps: 1) facing up to life's brevity, and 2) facing up to the truth about my physical condition. The truth was staring me in the face from those photographs. And the truth was what was going to finally set me free.

My resolve to get healthy was strong, but the practical application of my good intentions was sometimes difficult. I attempted a complete eating/exercise program. And failed. Failed miserably. A couple of my friends said the program was a failure. My nagging inner voice tried to tell me that I was a failure.

But in retrospect, I don't think either the program or my personal resolve was the root of the failure. I think I simply bit off more than I could chew at one time.

For more ideas on instituting lasting life changes, see the chapter in this book on Successful New Year's Resolutions (Chapter 8). The principles outline there can be used at any time of year when you're ready to make changes, not just January 1st.

21

USING UP LEFTOVERS

Leftovers. We all have them, don't we? But what do we do with them?

I don't really like keeping them in my refrigerator until a science project on mold develops, but sometimes it's hard to know what to use leftovers for without driving the family crazy. I don't care to hear another chorus of that all-too-familiar song, "What?! Meatloaf... AGAIN?!"

Probably the most important step with leftovers is making sure to keep them safe. We're not really saving any money on our family budget if that frugal dinner of leftovers sends everyone to the hospital with food poisoning!

To keep leftovers safe, cover and refrigerate within two hours of a meal, freeze to keep more than three days, and thaw frozen leftovers in the refrigerator.

I try to plan one meal each week to use up leftovers. Often it's during a lunchtime with just the kids and I, but sometimes there's enough food to feed the entire family. A complete meal of food that's been "found" in the refrigerator is like getting an extra meal each week for free.

It's a good idea to try and change the way the leftover is served from one meal to the next. Rather than serving leftover fried chicken, you could take the meat off the bone and prepare cold chicken sandwiches for a change of pace.

Suggestions for Using Leftovers

- Bread (loaf ends, slices starting to dry). Use in bread pudding, French toast, meat loaf extender, croutons, stuffing, bread crumbs

- Egg (hard-cooked). Use in casseroles, salads, sandwiches.

- Fruit (fresh, canned or frozen). Use in smoothies, milk shakes, gelatin desserts, cobblers, fruit bread, muffins, jam, freezer pops.

- Meat, poultry, or fish (cooked). Use in soups, stew, salad, quiche, enchiladas, stir fry, sandwiches, pot pies.

- Potatoes (cooked). Use in meat pies, salads, soups, stew.

- Rice or pasta (cooked). Use in casseroles, soups.

- Vegetables (cooked). Use in casseroles, quiche, salads, soups, sprinkled over a baked potato, in pot pies.

Pancakes, French toast, or waffles can just be popped into a sealed bag in your freezer. When you have enough assorted breakfast leftovers to make a meal, each person can have a variety of different items. To reheat, toast in the toaster on the Pastry setting.

Coffee and tea can be frozen in ice cube trays, then transfer the frozen coffee/tea cubes to plastic freezer bags. These work well for iced coffee or tea, and won't dilute the drink when the cubes melt.

Syrup drained from canned fruits can be mixed with a bit of milk and made into creamy freezer pops for a refreshing hot-weather treat. The leftover fruit syrup can also be frozen into cubes and used in cold summertime drinks.

If you make a lot of pie crusts, put the scraps into a plastic freezer bag. After collecting scraps for a while, you'll have enough for an extra crust.

Party Tray

One of the things our family does regularly with leftovers is to prepare a meal we call "Party Tray." I'll take all the collected leftovers out of the refrigerator and freezer, reheat them, and then divide the food items among our plates.

Everyone gets a little dab of this and a little dab of that—maybe only a bite or two of each item, but after the plate is filled with bits and pieces from past meals, it takes on the look of a plate from a party buffet line. I usually add some sliced cheese and crackers, plus a few cut-up fresh veggies, to complete the party theme.

My kids love this Party Tray meal idea. I hesitated for a long time to serve Party Tray to my husband, but one Saturday I just threw together a Party Tray meal for lunch. I was so surprised—my husband thought it was a great idea and wanted to know why I didn't do this when he was around. So Party Tray became a regular event, enjoyed by the whole family.

Soup and Bread Night

One night each week we have a Soup and Bread night. I'll either bake a loaf of fresh bread, a bunch of hearty rolls, or a big pan of cornbread. I keep a covered bucket in the freezer for storing assorted leftovers (meats, vegetables, rice, beans, etc.) to make soup.

One woman told me she drew a lady's face on the soup bucket and called the lady the Freezer Fairy. Her children could hardly wait to feed their leftovers to the Freezer Fairy. Each week, they were excited to see what delicious soup she was going to make for their family. By the way, the Freezer Fairy's magic doesn't work well on fish, so don't add leftover fish to your soup bucket in the freezer.

Happy frugal eating!

22

CRISIS MEAL PLANNING

If your home is anything like mine, you've probably found that five o'clock each evening is one of the most hectic times of the day. Mom and dad are just finishing up a long day of work at home or at the office. The kids are hungry and tired after a full day of school and afternoon sports. It's time to fix supper or at least we should be getting dinner started if we want to eat a meal before midnight!

But what's for dinner tonight?

Well, your guess is probably as good as mine, and it seems like more often than not, nobody knows! So the whole family hops into the car and heads through the local drive-thru for the third time this week.

Someone I know once called it "crisis meal

planning." Each night's dinner is the latest in a string of mealtime crisis management decisions. Everyone's tired. The kids are hungry. The whining has started in earnest. What's a parent to do?

Rather than planning ahead to prevent panic and poor nutritional choices, many families coast through their day without giving a thought to dinner, and then discover that they've crashed headlong into that nightly mealtime crisis once again.

Cooking ahead for the freezer can be the answer to this all-too-frequent mealtime dilemma. I've discovered as people become more adept and experienced at cooking for the freezer, they often switch from doing a full one-day-each-month cooking frenzy to using a simpler process referred to as "mini-sessions."

A mini-session consists of choosing one main ingredient, such as chicken, and then preparing a group of chicken recipes in a single afternoon or evening. A mini-session usually involves only an hour or two of cooking rather than the eight to ten hours often required for a complete month of cooking.

By waiting for main ingredients to go on sale at your local market, you can stock up on large quantities and take advantage of great prices.

For example, if you stock up on lean ground beef at this week's sale, a relatively short mini-session could easily supply you with five to ten ground beef meals tucked away in the freezer. When chicken goes on sale later in the month, you can add another five to ten meals to your personal stash of Frozen Assets.

Simply by purchasing and cooking in bulk as you follow the sale flyers from the grocery store, you can save a great deal of time and money without ever investing an entire day in a monthly cooking session.

If you're looking for some introductory information on freezer meal cooking, be sure to check out one of my *Frozen Assets* cookbooks and stop by my Frozen Assets webpage at: FrozenAssets.info

23

SAVING ON MEAL EXPENSES

How much of your family's hard earned money goes to groceries? $150 per week? $100? Believe it or not, it's relatively simple to spend as little as $75 per week on groceries for a family of four. But slashing the food bill down to those lower numbers means you may need to rethink the way your family eats.

For today's busy families, it's often easier to swing by the local drive-thru restaurant rather than finding time and energy to cook a new meal every night. Not only is fast food an expensive alternative for feeding your family, it's also not the healthiest way to eat on a regular basis. If this describes your dinner-time dilemma, you're not alone.

Keep ingredients on hand for several quick and easy meals.

Cook some of your meals ahead to store in the freezer for easy preparation later in the week. For an easy way to build up a stash of frozen assets, you can simply double and triple recipes now and then as you go about your regular cooking during the week. By stockpiling the extra meals in the freezer, all you'll need to do is heat a meal and make a side dish or salad for one of those all-too-frequent busy nights with no time to cook. By cooking ahead, you can also save money by purchasing ingredients in bulk and taking advantage of sales at the market.

Occasionally serve breakfast for dinner. Even when prepared in a big way, breakfast is one of the most economical meals to make. In many busy homes, families rarely have time for a big breakfast of pancakes, eggs, and bacon in the morning, so it's a special treat to have a meal like that for dinner now and then. An omelet also makes a good dinner choice.

Simplifying Food Prep

By planning and preparing bigger meals at dinner-time, you can use the leftovers for lunches brought from home rather than buying lunch at work every day.

Have one night each week where your children are each responsible for dinner for the entire family. This can be as simple as opening a can of soup and fixing grilled cheese sandwiches.

Crockery cookers are great for easy dinner prep—just throw the ingredients into the crock in the morning and dinner's waiting when you get home.

Planning Ahead

Even if you don't think cooking for an entire month would be of interest to you or your family, planning your meals ahead of time can really simplify meal planning during the month, and also save money.

First, set your grocery budget and then make the menus and grocery list fit your budget—not the other way around. Decide what you can afford to spend and don't go over that. You'd be surprised how creative you can be when you know you can only spend "this much and no more" at the store.

Take a few minutes to make a monthly menu and write down just what you need in the house for each meal. Go through the freezer and the cabinets to take stock of what you have on hand already. Then look at your calendar to see what the monthly activities are—for example make note of any birthday dinners, evenings when everyone will be leaving the house for the evening so you'll need a quick meal, times you're eating at someone else's home, or whatever events would affect your meal planning for the month.

Then take a look at the sale flyers for your local grocery stores. To save the most money, plan your meals around what's on sale and what you already have on hand. If you plan to shop weekly, make up all your individual weekly grocery lists for the month ahead of time (write up the entire month of shopping lists in one day so all you'll need to do is run to the store when it's time to shop).

Write out your meal plan on a blank calendar page and hang it in an easily visible spot (on the refrigerator, on a family bulletin board, etc.). It takes time to make out the menu and grocery lists, but it saves even more time every day and causes much less stress when the decision is already made about what's for supper that night.

Food Co-Ops / Bulk Buying

Be sure to check in your local areas for food buying co-ops. Many have small membership fees that you'll quickly recoup from the significant savings you're able to receive on many commonly purchased items. Natural food co-ops are common and a great way to purchase organic fruits and vegetables, whole grains and other expensive items at competitive prices.

Some communities offer a food buying program called Share. For a minimum charge (usually about $14) and 2 hours community service, participants receive a box of food valued at $35-$40. The community service can be something as simple as helping an elderly neighbor or working in your church nursery or Sunday School. The Share programs often offer meatless shares as well as the standard grocery items.

You can also start your own little unofficial food bulk buying co-op with a group of friends or neighbors. By purchasing items like flour, sugar, cream of wheat, oats, etc., in large bulk containers (50 pounds), you can then divide up the item into family-sized amounts, and split the cost.

Many people purchase large quantities of items from their local club store. While many of the items at these stores can be found at tremendous savings, be sure to shop comparatively even here. Sometimes you'll find that the sale at your local corner grocery store will actually be less expensive per pound or per item than the prices at the big warehouse stores. Always bring a calculator with you so you can make sure you're really getting the best price per unit.

Also, be sure to only buy in quantity those items that you're sure you'll be using before they go bad. Stockpiling toilet paper is a good idea since it's one of those items you know you'll be using eventually. Stockpiling bananas on sale might not be such a good idea since they spoil quickly—unless you're planning on baking with them, or freezing banana pulp to use in recipes later.

General Grocery Tips

- Buy ground beef on sale and divide up into smaller portions for casseroles etc. Freeze until ready to use.
- Grate your own cheese, rather than buying it already grated. Also, purchasing cheese in large quantities, grating it, and then freezing for later use is a great way to save time and money.
- Avoid pre-packaged whenever possible. Make

your own individually packaged puddings, applesauce, yogurts, etc.

- Buy produce in season.
- Avoid the gourmet-type stuff.

If your kids want pop, chips, candy etc. have them buy their own. This will help to limit how much of that they will buy, plus they will begin to learn the value of money.

24

WINNING THE GROCERY GAME

Trying to save money on groceries? It can be almost like a game as you look for ways to outsmart the supermarket. Try these ideas for starters:

1. Buy cheese in large quantities on sale. Grate the cheese and freeze in zip-top freezer bags. To use, just take out the amount of cheese you need (bang the bag on the countertop if frozen together), and keep the rest frozen.

2. Give store brands a try. If you find a tasty, high quality store brand or generic product, you'll discover the prices are often 20-50% below similar name brand products.

3. Think of meat as a side dish or condiment and serve in smaller portions. Fill up on salads and vegetables instead.

4. Buy large packages of pretzels, chips and other snack items on sale. Re-package them in small zip-top bags or wrapped in plastic wrap to pop into lunches.

5. When cake mix boxes are on sale, stock up. Bake several, cut into serving-sized pieces, then freeze individually for easy lunchtime desserts.

6. Don't buy non-food items at the grocery store. These items can usually be purchased elsewhere for less money.

7. Take your time shopping. It pays to examine labels, check cost per serving, compare brands, etc.

8. Check to see if your store offers any Preferred Shopper programs for loyal customers.

9. Shop at a local farmer's market for fresh fruit and vegetables.

10. Watch closely as the cashier rings up your groceries with an electronic scanner. Occasionally

the scanner will come up with the wrong price. Some stores will give you incorrectly scanned items for free.

11. Get a Rain Check from the store if an advertised item is out of stock.

12. Ask the store manager if you can browse through their dented can selection. Stores often sell diapers and other products for a discount if the bags have been ripped or opened.

13. If anything you buy is spoiled, return it.

14. Paper products can run up your "food" bill. Use cloth kitchen towels and napkins, laundering them frequently.

15. Buy produce in season and on sale.

16. Buy grains, flours, sugars and dry beans from a grocery warehouse or food co-op.

17. When purchasing pre-bagged produce (apples, oranges, potatoes, etc.), weigh several to find the heaviest bag. They sometimes vary by as much as a pound.

18. Substitute turkey ham and turkey sausages in recipes.

19. Keep ingredients on hand for several quick and easy meals. When time is scarce, you won't be as tempted to run out to the local drive-thru for a fast meal. Storing prepared meals in your freezer helps with this, too.

20. Turkey is usually a better value per pound than chicken. Substitute cooked turkey in your cooked chicken recipes, and use leftover turkey for sandwiches and casseroles.

25

MORE SIMPLE WAYS TO SAVE ON GROCERIES

Groceries are one of the few flexible items in a family budget, but it can sometimes be challenging to find creative ways to save on regular family food costs. The following are some simple tips for reducing your grocery expenses. If you're a long-time pro at frugal living, some of these may be old hat, but I'm amazed at how many people still find these types of tips helpful.

1. Plan ahead.

    Whether you're cooking your meals ahead of time to store in the freezer, or just planning your menu and shopping lists in advance, it helps to know what you're going to eat, and when. With fewer last minute food-related decisions, this also helps keep your family away from developing a first-name relationship with the pizza delivery guy! (And your own home cooking is probably a lot healthier than the pizza guy's wares, anyway.)

2. Set your grocery budget and then make sure your menu and grocery list fits your budget.

   Don't plan on eating Chicken Cordon Bleu tonight if your budget only allows for rice and beans. And don't let yourself give into a pity party, thinking, "We can only eat rice and beans tonight. Boo hoo!" Rice and beans are good food! Just think how healthy your family (and your budget!) will be.

3. Plan your meals around items you already have on hand.

   Also plan around the sale flyers from your local grocery stores. But be warned: Moderation in all things.

   One time I found ground turkey on sale for four pounds for a dollar. Well, being the good little frugal person that I am, I bought forty pounds. Forty pounds?! Yikes! Do you have any idea how sick and tired my family got of ground turkey?

I tried sneaking it into spaghetti sauce, casseroles, meat balls, you name it. Before they'd take a bite, someone in the family would always ask (with their nose crinkled up funny), "Is it turkey, Mom?" Now please understand—my family likes ground turkey. In moderation. But too much of a good thing is ... well, too much of a good thing.

4. Shop with cash.

This is a surprisingly effective means of staying on budget. Somehow writing a check seems less "concrete" than paying cash, making it easier to spend more than intended. Keep a running total of how much you're spending at the store. If you find that you're about to spend more than you had budgeted for that trip, put items back and re-shop for better bargains.

5. Keep a Price Diary.

List all regularly purchased items (food, toiletries, paper products, etc.) in a small notebook small enough to slip into your purse or pocket when you go shopping. When you're browsing through store advertisements or doing your actual shopping, write down (in pencil!) the lowest price you see for each item listed in your Price Diary (change the prices when you see lower prices than you've already written in the notebook). This way you'll know for sure if a sale price is low enough to make it worth stocking up.

6. While shopping, "Look high, look low."

Stores often place the most expensive items at eye level. Don't be embarrassed to crawl around on your hands and knees in the grocery store looking for bargains. You might get some funny looks from other shoppers, but the cashiers will be amazed at how much food you're buying for so little money. And the look of approval you'll give yourself in the mirror when you've stayed within your budget is worth a few laughs in the store, believe me!

7. Beware of displays at the end of aisle (aka: "end caps").

The advertised special they're highlighting might be a good buy, but the item will often be displayed with non-sale (and very expensive!) products to entice you into impulse purchases. "Oh, look! Spaghetti sauce is on sale. Now, let's see … to go with the sauce, I'll just grab some of these handy packages of gourmet pasta … and this expensive container of Parmesan cheese … and these cute little imported canned mushrooms … and this lovely bottle of French wine … and

..." Well, you get the idea. Just say, "No!"

8. Buy Loss Leaders.

Sometimes a store will offer what's known as Loss Leaders—those items the store will sell so cheaply, they'll actually take a loss on each sale. They're hoping to entice new customers into the store who will then purchase other items in addition to the sale item. You need to hold strong against impulse purchases in these situations.

Just run into the store, buy the Loss Leaders, don't do any browsing, and get out of there fast before temptation strikes—or you may find your best laid money-saving plans way-laid by cute little floral arrangements for the upcoming holiday.

9. Use coupons wisely.

Only use coupons for those items and brands that you would normally purchase. And always check the expiration date on your coupons. Some stores offer double coupons. Check with your favorite store and see if they do. Some stores will even accept competitor's coupons. Hand your coupons to the cashier before they start to ring up your order so you don't forget later.

10. Buy in bulk.

Stock up on frequently used items when they go on sale (canned goods, toilet paper, shampoo, etc.). Only bulk buy those items you know you'll use before they go bad. Stockpiling toilet paper is a good idea, but bananas might be another story (unless you plan on baking with them or freezing the pulp for use in recipes later).

11. Shop the local co-op.

Natural food co-ops are becoming quite common. This can be a great way to purchase organic fruits and vegetables, whole grains and other usually expensive items at competitive prices.

12. Watch for sales on lean ground meats.

Divide the meat into one pound batches and freeze in individual re-sealable freezer bags. (But remember my story about the forty pounds of ground turkey! Repeat after me: Moderation in all things … moderation in all things.)

13. Set a price goal.

One simple approach to meal planning is setting a price goal for each meal. For example: Breakfast = $0.50 per person, Dinner = $3-4 total.

14. Don't shop when you're hungry.

    You're more liable to make impulse buys when your stomach's rumbling.

15. Look for sales.

    Check store entrances or bulletin boards for special flyers, and don't forget to look in local newspapers for additional coupons.

16. Shop the edges of store.

    For the healthiest and freshest foods, shop the perimeter of the supermarket. Dairy, meat and produce departments are usually located around the outer walls, while you'll find those pre-packaged "food" (and I use the term "food" lightly) items located in the center of the store.

17. Avoid going down the aisles.

    These are not only less healthy spots for buying food, but they're also the location of many impulse buys. Did you really need that box of chocolate- covered frozen cream puffs? If you would've stayed on the perimeter, you wouldn't have even seen those tempting cream puffs.

26

SUPER SIMPLE, SUPER CHEAP RECIPES

I'm always on the lookout for super-simple, super-cheap recipes for lunches, snacks and using up leftovers. I usually do okay with dinner (there's almost always something tasty hiding in my freezer), but sometimes I run out of ideas for the other eating times during the day, especially on those busy days with little time to cook.

A couple of simple things we do:

"Tortilla Roll-Ups" - Just spread cream cheese and a couple slices of inexpensive sandwich meat onto a flour tortilla, roll up, and enjoy! I also add sprouts or lettuce if we have it around. A friend of mine slices the Roll-Ups into Pinwheels for variety — the Tortilla Pinwheels make a nice snack item for parties, too.

THE SIMPLE MOM'S IDEA BOOK

"World's Easiest Fruit Salad" - Fill a salad bowl with large cubes of fresh fruit (apples, oranges, bananas, melons, etc.), and then pour a carton of VANILLA-flavored yogurt (be sure NOT to use *plain* yogurt) over the fruit for a sauce. This is so simple, but very tasty.

"Pudding Pops" - Prepare a box of instant pudding according to instructions, pour into popcycle molds and freeze. If you use chocolate flavored pudding, you have super-simple do-it-yourself fudgesycles. Butterscotch pudding is really good this way, too.

"Mom's Goop"

Sometimes when there's "nothing to eat" around the house, it's possible to throw a dab of this and a dab of that into a pot, and end up with a delicious meal that would even make an Iron Chef proud.

Take the other night, for example, when I was feeling a bit like Old Mother Hubbard. "And when she got there, the cupboard was bare ..." I rummaged around in the cupboards and dark recesses of my refrigerator and freezer, and wound up throwing together the following:

- 2 lbs. of pre-cooked ground beef hiding in my freezer
- a chopped onion and a bit of garlic

- a zucchini, quartered length-wise and sliced
- a second small zucchini, grated (to thicken the mixture)
- two cans of Mexican-style stewed tomatoes
- about half a cup of salsa

I threw everything together into a large saucepan and cooked it all until the veggies softened and the flavors had a chance to blend.

In the meantime, I boiled up some broken pieces of lasagna noodles from an opened bag I found cluttering up the bottom of my pantry shelf, and then I glopped the ground beef mixture on top of the hot cooked noodles.

I sprinkled the whole mess with grated cheddar cheese, gooped on some sour cream, and then everyone—even my pickiest family member—ate it with gusto. They even asked if we could have it again sometime. Well, sure kids. Next time there's nothing to eat, we'll eat it again. But I supposed I'd better come up with a more appetizing name than "Mom's Goop."

Simple Times Readers' Suggestions

The following are some tips and simple recipes submitted by Simple Times' readers.

Submitted by: Angel
1) For lunches, stuff a pita pocket with green salad (and shredded cheese if you have it), and then top

the whole thing with ranch dressing.

2) For snacks, spread cream cheese on a slice of salami and add a stuffed olive, roll it up and insert a toothpick in it to hold it together.

3) Another snack that I make: top a graham cracker with cake frosting (my favorite is chocolate!). Yummy!

4) Cut a cantaloupe in half and fill with cottage cheese.

5) There are wonderful and usually very economical recipes at the "Taste Of Home" web-page. I think their address is: Reimanpublications.com

Submitted by: Jim
Take a can of cheap spaghetti sauce and a can of black beans, heat together and serve over pasta.

Submitted by: Ronnie
Apple slices with peanut butter… yummy, cheap and easy.

Submitted by: Lynne T.
Serve leftover chili on top of leftover rice. Makes a "Red Beans and Rice" type of meal.

Submitted by: Susan A.
I prepare a box of macaroni and cheese, and heat a can of chili. Then I serve the chili scooped over the macaroni. Using leftover homemade chili makes this even more economical and a great deal healthier, but you asked for

cheap and "easy" ideas so I immediately thought of this simple recipe just using boxes and cans.

Submitted by: Marilyn

Perfect Oatmeal: 1 cup of water, 1/2 cup of regular oatmeal, a dash of salt and 3 minutes in the microwave equals perfect oatmeal. I came up with this after much trial-and-error looking for that "perfect" proportion of ingredients.

ABOUT THE AUTHOR

Deborah Taylor-Hough is the author of several books including: *Frugal Living For Dummies®*, the best-selling *Frozen Assets* cookbook series, and *A Simple Choice: A practical guide for saving your time, money and sanity.*

Deborah is a graduate of the University of Washington, and is currently in Graduate School pursuing a Master of Fine Arts (MFA) in Creative Writing. She has worked as the Outreach Director and Youth Director at her church, and teaches workshops and seminars throughout the USA and Canada.

Her workshop topics include:

- living within your means
- simple living
- cooking for the freezer
- general homemaking
- writing, publishing and publicity
- identifying personal priorities
- simplifying the holidays
- common sense home education
- ... and more!

Visit Deborah online: TheSimpleMom.com

Also available from Deborah Taylor-Hough

Frozen Assets: Cook for a Day, Eat for a Month
ISBN: 9781402218590 (Sourcebooks)

This breakthrough cookbook delivers a program for readers to cook a week or month's worth of meals in just one day by using easy and affordable recipes to create a customized meal plan. The author, who saved $24,000 on her family's total grocery bill during a five-year period, offers up kid-tested and family-approved recipes in *Frozen Assets*, plus bulk-cooking tips for singles, shopping lists, recipes for two-week and 30-day meal plans, and a ten-day plan to eliminate cooking over the holidays. Cooking for the freezer allows you to plan ahead, purchase items in bulk, cut down on waste, and stop those all-too-frequent trips to the drive-thru.

Frozen Assets Lite and Easy
ISBN: 9781402218606 (Sourcebooks)

Taylor-Hough is back with a book of low-fat, lower-calorie meal plans that use the same time-saving and cost-effective methods. *Frozen Assets Lite and Easy* shows readers how to be healthy while still saving time and money, with shopping lists, recipes, and detailed instruction on how to make freezer cooking work for you.

Frugal Living For Dummies®
ISBN: 9780764554032 (Wiley)

Need help keeping that New Year's resolution to eliminate credit card debt and live within your means? Packed with tips on cutting costs on everything from groceries to gifts for all occasions, this practical guide shows you how to spend less on the things you need and save more for those fun things you want.

A Simple Choice: A practical guide for saving your time, money and sanity
ISBN: 9781891400490 (SourceBooks)

The number one complaint of people today is the lack of meaning in their hectic lives. In this book, the author addresses societal emptiness and the personal search for contentment. *A Simple Choice* not only examines the futility of keeping up with the Jones', but depicts the simple joy and fulfillment of keeping up with ourselves. Through practical help in the areas of homemaking, family unity, saving money, simple spending plans, easy and frugal cooking, and much more, Taylor-Hough guides us down a simpler life path. In an era of self-reflection, *A Simple Choice* holds the answers to life's simple joys, available to everyone.

To order these and other titles go to:
TheSimpleMom.com

Praise for the Author's Books

for: *Frozen Assets: Cook for a Day, Eat for a Month*

"Finally, a realistic way to combine the cost-effectiveness of cooking from scratch with the convenience of quick and easy meals!"
–Mary Hunt, editor/publisher of the Cheapskate Monthly

"*Frozen Assets* will prove to be the hands-down authority on once-a-month cooking."
–Susan Sands, publisher Home Words magazine

"This title is bound to be a favorite … because of its comprehensive scope and easy-going style."
–Christian Parenting Today

"This book offers relief to those tired of eating restaurant fare or expensive, over packaged convenience foods at the end of a hard day."
–Library Journal

"…offers kid-tested recipes that are easy and affordable."
–The Oregonian

"… details a plan for cooking and freezing in quantity, with grocery lists, shopping lists, storage tips and dollar-stretching hints. The recipes are simple and straightforward, using everyday ingredients."
–Atlanta Journal

for: *Frugal Living For Dummies®*

"A must-have for those wanting more out of their money!"
–Jonni McCoy, author of *Miserly Moms*

"Saving money has never been this simple!"
–Gary Foreman, editor/founder of The Dollar Stretcher

for: *A Simple Choice: A practical guide for saving your time, money and sanity*

"If you think you have learned all you need to know about living simply, think again. *A Simple Choice* offers new insights, refreshing common sense and the author's firsthand experience ... don't hesitate on this one—many delightful discoveries await you!"
–Linda Breen Pierce, author of *Choosing Simplicity: Real People Finding Peace and Fulfillment in a Complex World*

"Taylor-Hough does a fine job of meshing the practical with the philosophical. Those seeking a simpler lifestyle need to hear more than just the 'whys', but also the 'hows' of simplification. Deborah does this in a way that's palatable and easy to digest, for both beginners and veteran simplifiers alike."
–Nancy Twigg, author of *Celebrate Simply*

❦

www.ingramcontent.com/pod-product-compliance
Lightning Source LLC
Chambersburg PA
CBHW060511030426
42337CB00015B/1842